LIVERPOOL
OVERHEAD
RAILWAY

Acknowledgments

Dedicated to Mrs.Gladys Box for her invaluable help and kindness.

Special thanks are due to Duncan Gomersall for his continued assistance and enthusiasm. Also to Brian Hilton and Ken Longbottom, both sadly no longer with us and missed by all who benefited from their encouragement, wit and counsel.

I am also indebted to the following people and organisations whose contributions have made this book possible.

Frank Barr, William Barr, the late Charles Box, Crich Tram Museum, John Gahan, the late Ken Green, Bernard Matthews, Jim Peden, the late Rev. Denys Rokeby, Ernest Simkins, John F.Ward, Derek Whale, Colin Wilkinson, Crosby Library, Liverpool Libraries, Liverpool Nautical Research Group, Merseyside Maritime Museum and Stations U.K.

Front cover This design was used for at least 20 years first appearing in the 1930s under the direction of W.L.Box (manager 1934-1943) as did this copy. Revised prices of up to 1/8d and 1/4d together with his successor's name, H. Maxwell Rostron, were pasted over the original details and used up to the end of the line.

©1997 Paul Bolger

Published by:
The Bluecoat Press
Liverpool

ISBN 1 872568 40 8

Printed in Spain by:
GZ Printek, Bilbao

Design and typesetting by:
March Design
Liverpool

Origination by:
Primary Four Limited, Moreton, Wirral.

LIVERPOOL
OVERHEAD
RAILWAY

Paul Bolger

The Bluecoat Press

Foreword

When Paul Bolger produced 'The Docker's Umbrella', his first illustrated book on the history of the Liverpool Overhead Railway, it was acclaimed with great interest and delight. Thousands of readers remembered the old scenes with nostalgia; but for countless others, perhaps unborn or too young when the railway was finally closed for demolition in 1956, it has simply remained a waterfront legend associated with Liverpool's golden era of maritime history and with little or nothing to mark it's passing.

Paul then took us on a grand south-bound journey, starting at Seaforth and ending at Dingle's underground station – an education in itself.

Continuing the story in this second book, 'LIVERPOOL OVERHEAD RAILWAY', we board the train again to rumble back along the northbound, opposite track, of this fabulous 'railway in the sky' ... the 'Ovee' as it was locally dubbed. The author has added a collection of over ninety fascinating – mostly unpublished photographs, including once well known sites and landmarks, where we stop to ponder en route, to capture a realistic atmosphere through the decades. With their interesting, explanatory captions this must surely complete the most comprehensive pictorial record of the railway. All aboard? Then let's go.

Derek Whale

This poster hails from the period of S.B.Cottrell, the first general manager and engineer of the line (1893–1908). Although not a masterpiece it was an eye-catching design and one of the first to publicise the railway's virtues.

THE LIVERPOOL
OVERHEAD
RAILWAY
A SPLENDID VIEW OF THE DOCKS & RIVER.
FIRST & FASTEST
ELECTRIC
(OVERHEAD) RAILWAY
IN THE WORLD.
RAPID AND FREQUENT SERVICE
OF SALOON CARS AT
CHEAP FARES
Affording Magnificent Panoramic View
OF THE LIVERPOOL DOCKS
• 6½ miles in extent •
AND THE RIVER MERSEY.
31, JAMES ST LIVERPOOL.
S.B. COTTRELL M.Inst.C.E.
ENGINEER & GENERAL MANAGER.
THE LIVERPOOL PRINTING & STATIONERY Co LIMITED

Introduction

As you might expect, the publication of 'The Docker's Umbrella' (Bluecoat Press, 1992) unearthed many more photographs of the line and surrounding area. Initial thoughts were for a second edition but, as preparations were underway, it became apparent there was enough fresh material to warrant a separate volume. It was also deemed fitting that publication should follow the centenary of the opening of the last part of the railway, namely the extension to Dingle Station in December 1896. The theme of the first book was a journey from north to south with the emphasis on the line itself – this time we shall travel in the opposite direction with surrounding locations featured more prominently to enhance the flavour of the different decades we will encounter along the route.

So, we're off to Dingle. Grab your tickets, secure a window seat and enjoy a return journey on the Liverpool Overhead Railway.

Paul Bolger, 1996

Another Cottrell-period poster but the vintage of this one is most definitely 1906 as 'Captains Lane' (later Ford) station did not open until then. Added to which the company's connections to the LYR were completed by that year and both railways would have lost no time in advertising such a service. The presence of Neachell's name who was the manager between 1908–1926, is misleading. These adverts were used well into the second managerial dynasty and rather than reprint the whole poster they merely superimposed 'E.J. Neachell' stickers over Cottrell's name as is the case here.

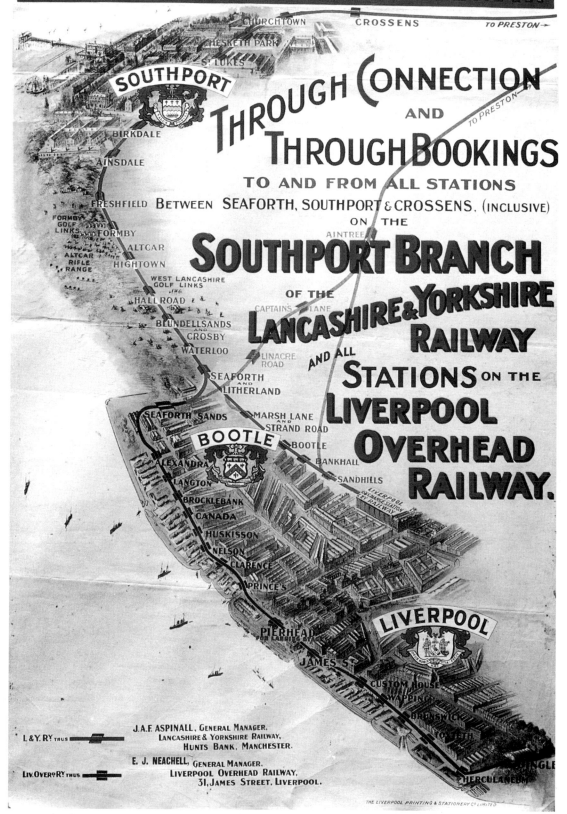

Liverpool Overhead Railway was not just a railway, it was an institution, an unforgettable experience for those fortunate to have travelled on it. The world's first elevated electric railway running from Seaforth to Dingle, it offered passengers unrivalled views of the city and its docks. Trains commenced in 1893 and for the next sixty years the 'Ovee' was an essential part of the transport network, giving fast and efficient access to the miles of docks that lined its route.

Forced to close because of the cost of necessary repairs, the last trains rumbled past disbelieving crowds on Sunday, 30 December 1956. The Overhead Railway had passed into history.

Dingle Station c.1906

1900 The approach to Dingle from the foot of Park Road leaves no doubt as to the nature of the building on the left – note also the gaslamp which bears the legend 'Tramway Station'.

Opposite top 1956 Before entering, the traveller might be tempted to buy something for the journey at McLachlans kiosk. A sign above advertises that travel on the Overhead was still the cheapest with a third-class single to Pier Head a mere 4d (7d return). Further savings were possible with weekly and monthly season tickets on offer at 4/9d and 18/- respectively.

Opposite bottom First Class carraige interior.

Left top 1956 to reach the island platform, travellers had to negotiate a white-washed access tunnel and descend a set of stairs.

Left bottom 1938 The opposite side of the platform looking in the other direction. A rumbling noise heralds the arrival of a train from Seaforth into the underground chamber. In a few minutes time, the train will return north. The signal box which controls train movements at this station can be seen at the far end of the platform.

LIVERPOOL OVERHEAD RAILWAY CO.

Station.. (Up or Down)....................

..................day the..........of............................... 19..........

REMITTED THIS DAY

	£	s.	d.
Pound Notes			
10/- „			
Cheques			
Silver			
Copper			
Amount Collected by Cashier ...			
TOTAL CASH ...			
Army Warrants			
Navy Warrants			
Port Labour Warrants			
Other Warrants			
*TOTAL CASH AND WARRANTS ...			

PARTICULARS OF ABOVE

Remitted for Traffic as per Daily Return			
Left Luggage (...............................)			
Lost Property (...............................)			
Agency, Bicycle Stall Rents, etc.—			
....			
....			
....			
Credit Deducted for			
Debit Paid for			

TOTAL OF PARTICULARS (must agree with *)

Signature of
Clerk in Charge..

Opposite top 1956 Once underway, it is not long before daylight can be seen rapidly punctuated with the latticework of Herculaneum bridge as the train emerges from Dingle tunnel. Below and to the left is Herculaneum Dock with coal wagons at the quayside.

Opposite bottom 1956 Clearing the bridge, the lights inside the carriages are extinguished as the train curves right and begins to slow for the first stop at Herculaneum. Cashier Mr.Adcock is travelling alongside the driver to accept bags of station receipts handed in along the route. Each bag would have been accompanied by a completed remittance form (see blank reproduced here).

Below 1950s The train squeals to a halt at Herculaneum and we alight to take in the sights and sounds of the vicinity.

Opposite top 1956 On turning around and heading for the exit, one cannot help noticing the Herculaneum carriage shed which was once the southern terminus of the line prior to the 1896 extension to Dingle. Three-car sets are normally stored here in readiness for relief and rush-hour duties.

Opposite bottom 1955 Once at ground level, a flight of steps gives access to the Herculaneum footbridge which leads to lofty Grafton Street. The bridge is visible here between the deck of the Overhead and the tops of the 'Esso' tankers.

Above 1955 On the way to the footbridge looking north along the line of the Overhead. Tank wagons are a common sight here as a great deal of oil is landed and stored pending distribution. Being completely surrounded by railways and docks, the peace is continually interrupted by the sounds of clanking wagons, engine noises and ships' hooters.

Above top 1953 Crossing the footbridge and with Herculaneum station in the distance, the now dishevelled Brunswick engine shed from Grafton Street can be seen below. Access to this depot was gained via a steep flight of steps situated a few yards north of the vantage point.

Above 1950s A short walk from Park Street brings us to the next Overhead station: Toxteth Dock with the huge ex-Cheshire Lines Railway warehouse towering above.

1950 keeping to the high ground and heading north towards Park Street via Horsfall and Caryl Streets. This skirts the boundary of the ex-Cheshire Lines Railway goods yard at Brunswick with its 40 ton travelling crane (pictured here) in operation. The rooftops on the left indicate the course of Caryl Street and the railway immediately below it is the main line from Liverpool Central.

Above top 1956 A modernised unit speeds past the Brunswick Dock on the left towards the station of the same name. The skyline on the landward side is dominated by modern tenement blocks.

Above 1950s Pulling into Brunswick Dock, notice the huge Coburg granary just beyond the left hand platform. Note also the relatively new station buildings, a post-war legacy of the Blitz.

Above top 1930s Brunswick twenty years earlier with its original buildings and colourful enamel notices. Adverts for Dewars, Schweppes, Stephens and Venos mingle with those for local businesses such as Arthur S.Porter of 33 Wapping (manufacturers of cloths, flags, bunting, ropes and twine), Condrons of 16 Esk Street (ship scalers) and Joseph Thompson & Co. of 22 Dutton Street (merchants for chains, cables and hawsers).

Above 1957 The next station along the line is Wapping, seen here from the roadway ten months after closure but still intact. In the distance are the dock warehouses of the same name.

Above 1940 A little further, on to the right, can be seen the devastation wreaked upon the ex-London & North Western Railway's massive Wapping goods station by enemy bombing. Also known as Park Lane, it was never rebuilt to its former size and carried on 'business as usual' until final closure in 1965. This historic site dated back to the pioneering days of the Liverpool & Manchester Railway Company which opened a depot here in 1830.

Opposite top 1950s The next stop is Canning which was known as Custom House prior to 1945. We shall take leave of the train once more to inspect the dockside activity.

Opposite bottom 1940s Canning Dock with four sizeable vessels at rest together with a number of sailing barges. This was originally the entrance basin for Liverpool's first dock, the Old Dock, built in 1719 and filled in 1826. Canning then became a dock in its own right and was named after George Canning, the Liverpool MP, in 1829.

Above 1956 Skirting Salthouse Dock to the connecting bridge with Albert Dock, where two buoys are receiving attention just inside the latter.

Opposite top 1956 A short walk around the corner is the Albert Dock quadrangle, constructed in 1846 by Jesse Hartley. A coaster *Nora Cooper* is the nearest vessel and beyond its funnel, the Dock Master's office can be seen.

Opposite bottom 1951 *Ranger* of the Liverpool & Glasgow Salvage Co. and a concrete barge (or 'flat') occupy the north eastern corner of Albert Dock. The latter vessel, with a hull actually made of concrete, was one of a number built during the last war due to the demand for conventional materials.

Right top 1952 A dredger in Canning Half Tide Basin has its cargo of waste sand extracted by grab-crane. When filtered and dried in the hoppers it was recycled for building purposes.

Right bottom 1956 Having retraced our steps to Canning Station we ascend the staircase headed 'Way In For Trains Going North'.

Opposite top 1956 The next leg of the journey shows a wide architectural variety of warehouses lined up in Strand Street to the right. We are approaching James Street, station where many travellers change to connect with trams, ferries or the underground Mersey Railway.

Opposite bottom 1951 Crossing to the opposite platform of James Street, a modernised unit enters with a Dingle train. Passengers change here for trains to Wirral. In the distance the Royal Liver Building dominates the skyline.

Above 1956 The James Street southbound platform provides an excellent view of the former White Star line building which was erected in 1898 in a style very similar to that of the original New Scotland Yard. This shipping line is famous for its ownership of the ill-fated *Titanic* and people's fears and superstitions thereafter were partly responsible for the company merging with Cunard in the 1930s. To the right of the building, the close proximity of the underground Mersey Railway's James Street station can be seen whilst, elsewhere, the impromptu car parks which sprang from cleared bomb-sites are much in evidence. The 'Kwik Snax' tea cabin in the immediate foreground seems as good a place as any for passengers to refresh themselves before continuing their journey on foot to the Pier Head.

Opposite top The walk from James Street takes us past the Goree Piazzas, large colonnaded warehouses first erected in 1793 and rebuilt in 1802 following a disastrous fire. Amongst the trades listed for these buildings in 1908 were ships chandlers, eating houses, corn merchants, wool brokers, licensed premises and team-owners (carthorses). This was not the place to be after nightfall as the sheltered walkway attracted vagrants, drunks and prostitutes. The warehouses were almost totally destroyed by enemy bombing and were pulled down after the war. This view clearly shows the Custom House in the distance, itself a wartime casualty. Bottom right are the last remains of Georges Dock which opened in 1771 and enlarged between 1822 and 1825 until it stretched from James Street to Chapel Street. Once the haunt of deep draught square rigged sailing ships and man o' war vessels, the dock was drained at the turn of the century and gradually filled in to make way for the Royal Liver, Cunard and Mersey Docks & Harbour Board buildings.

Opposite bottom c.1901 At the end of the colonnades we arrive at that part of the roadway called Georges Dock Gates where tramcars from the Pier Head briefly mingle with horse drawn through traffic.

Birdseye View of Liverpool (South).
Overhead Railway, Strand Street and Docks

Above top 1936 Thirty years on and Pier Head station is festooned with flags and bunting in celebration of George VI's coronation.

Above 1940s A view from the Royal Liver Buildings looking north along the river towards Wallasey and New Brighton. The Princes Dock West transit sheds are below and the red and black funnel of the cruiser berthed at the landing stage indicate it is one from the Cunard fleet. Sandwiched between the two is Riverside Station, where boat trains frequently disgorge hundreds of emigrants and troops.

1940s A glance further inland reveals Princes Dock in its entirety with six vessels berthed. This is largely the preserve of the Irish boats as is indicated by the advertisement. At the far end, note the bridge which boat trains cross as they wind their way to and from Riverside station.

Above 1940s A ninety degree turn to the right allows a view across the rooftops of the numerous warehouses that lie north of Chapel Street, many of which were operated by Henry Diaper & Co. The portal and roadway of the Mersey Tunnel Dock Branch dominate the scene whilst the Overhead is barely visible in the dark shadow cast by the Royal Liver Building.

Opposite top 1952 Pier Head tram terminus with its two large loops of trackwork and busy 'Green Goddesses'. Like the Overhead, the tram's days were numbered and the transition to buses was complete by 1957.

Opposite bottom 1950s Georges Landing Stage with its ferries and groups of people either waiting for their connection or strolling the deck taking in the sights and the bracing ozone. The choice of sailings from here and the Princes Stage further along was once extensive. Not only could one board vessels for America, Ireland and the Isle of Man but also day-trip pleasure cruises along the Mersey or to Blackpool, Llandudno and Anglesey. Added to which there were no fewer than eight different ferry crossings serving New Brighton, Egremont, Seacombe, Woodside, Rock Ferry, New Ferry and Eastham together with a vehicle/luggage steamer which plied to Birkenhead.

Right 1951 A manually operated departure clock and a poster advertising 'A New Thrill', namely the introduction of the 'Royal Iris' cruises on the May 2. The main attractions to this new service are billed as: *Dance to a first class orchestra on a grand pillarless dance deck; Fully licensed bars – smart cocktail bar and buffet; Fish and chip saloon; Glass enclosed fine observation deck; See the ever-changing panorama of a great sea port whilst you sail on in comfort.* This distinctive vessel which accommodated more than a thousand trippers became popular with locals and visitors alike and, being Liverpool, was not surprisingly given a down to earth nick-name – the 'Fish & Chip Boat'.

Opposite top 1952 *Bidston* arriving at the quayside.

Opposite bottom 1904 An early photograph before the creation of Liverpool's famous skyline. Work was underway on the Mersey Docks & Harbour Board structure which was the first of the trio to be completed in 1907. The Royal Liver Building followed in 1910 but the Cunard offices, the middle of the three, were not erected until after the 1914-18 war.

Above 1925 Once underway north again, on the left, a queue of traffic on the floating roadway that connected dry land with the Georges Landing Stage. The level of the roadway was dictated by the stage whose height fluctuated with the tide. All manner of vehicles used this thoroughfare but note especially the team of four shire horses necessary to haul a fully laden dray up the gradient at low tide.

Opposite top 1951 The remains of Princes station, closed in 1941 due to enemy action, is passed as Princes Half Tide Basin briefly comes into view. Pictured in that dock is *Marchmont* of the Marchmont Steamship Co. loading sacks at the landward quayside.

Opposite bottom 1953 The next expanse of water is East Waterloo Dock but one of the massive grain warehouses which stand east and west of it rapidly interrupts the view. The dock was laid out in 1834 followed in 1867 by the warehouses which were fully equipped to raise, store, turn, ventilate and discharge grain. Note the chimneys of Clarence Dock Power Station in the distance; these were commonly referred to as the 'Three Ugly Sisters'.

Opposite top 1950s We are is met at Clarence Dock station by a southbound service and a horde of waiting dock workers and other travellers.

Opposite bottom 1931 From the top of Clarence Dock station steps, the view of the generating station which goes by the same name can be admired. It occupies the site of the filled-in dock and although not yet fully constructed, the rows of laden and unladen hopper wagons prove it is operating in some capacity. Note the rail weighbridges in the foreground which record the amount of coal each hopper carries.

Above 1951 At ground level, carthorses are everywhere and greatly outnumber the motor and steam lorries which were to eventually replace them. Four take a well earned rest here whilst one of Mr.Diaper's warehouses is stocked with merchandise.

Above top 1954 One of the castellated gatehouses which are a common feature of the dock road. This particular one with its studded door and cell-like interior dates from the 1820s, before the abolition of slavery and at a time when the Liverpool & Manchester Railway was still in the planning stage.

Above 1950s We climb the steps to the next station on the line, Nelson Dock. Ahead lies that part of the line known as the 'switchback' where the tracks plunged underneath the high-level coal railway.

Above top 1950s As the train descends the gradient, the view to the right shows the bridge which carried the high level coal railway across the dock road towards Bramley-Moore dock. The towers at each corner housed winding gear which lifted the entire bridge when greater headroom was required by large loads passing underneath.

Above 1941 Underneath the high-level coal railway, the train would then proceed up the incline and assume its elevated position. Here we see damage to this section a result of enemy action. The railway suffered its fair share of disruption during the Blitz and was forced to use buses on many occasions as a link between bombed sections. The Overhead was considered vital to the war effort and no time was wasted in restoring breaches. Note the huge ex-Midland Railway Sandon goods warehouse in the distance on the right.

Above top 1950s Normal service having been resumed, Huskisson is reached without incident. This was one of only two stations on the Overhead provided with footbridges over the line; the other was Gladstone. They were necessary to afford passage to and from the northbound platforms which stood immediately above dock property.

Above 1940s At ground level there is much to-ing and fro-ing between the docks and the three large LMS goods yards nearby, namely Sandon, Canada and Bankfield. Amongst the many sights is a 'Pug' working cab first trundling wagons along one of the dock-board lines which lie underneath the Overhead.

Above top 1941 Upon reaching the next venue, Canada, more destruction to this beloved line is witnessed – this time the side of a complete span crashed to ground level and the station buildings are heavily damaged.
Above 1958 Despite some sixteen months of closure, the rebuilt Canada still looked as though it was in business with no evidence of boarded-up staircases or other incapacity.

Above top 1950s Between Canada and Brocklebank stations, passengers are given the opportunity to fully appreciate the ships which have been getting noticeably larger since Huskisson.

Above 1930s On passing Canada and Brocklebank docks passengers are rewarded with fine views of vessels from the Pacific Steam Navigation Co., Elder Dempster and Royal Mail Lines.

Opposite top 1930s *Port Dunedin* operated by the Port Line, situated in the north east corner of Brocklebank Branch Dock.

Opposite bottom 1958 Brocklebank Station from the Dock Road.

Above 1956 Inside the Dock Estate at Brocklebank, an engine shed services the locomotives of the Mersey Docks & Harbour Board. We pay particular attention to MH&DB No.21 alongside the coaling platform, noting the spark arrester on its chimney with baffle plate above that. The latter was intended to keep the detrimental sulphurous blasts to a minimum when working underneath the Overhead's structure.

Opposite top 1955 Back on Regent Road and north of Nelson Street on the right we see the entrance of the old LNWR Alexandra Dock passenger terminus. The entrance to the ticket office is bricked up now as it booked its last traveller in 1948. This was the only mainline passenger station on the entire length of the dock road not counting Brunswick at the south end which closed in 1874. Alexandra continued to handle parcels traffic until 1967, note the British Railways three wheeled 'Scammel' articulated unit parked inside the gateway. During this period these nippy little vehicles were the mainstay of parcel distribution in towns and cities throughout the country.

Opposite bottom 1930 Twenty years earlier inside the dark train shed at Alexandra Dock passenger station. This view from the buffers shows the solitary platform curving right in the distance with wagons in the goods yard of the same name visible left.

Above top 1958 Further on past the large goods depot at Alexandra Dock was its Overhead namesake. This view from just inside the dock estate shows the tiny signal box between here and the station which was only pressed into service for emergencies such as failure of the automatic signals.

Above 1950s Whilst waiting at Alexandra for a northbound train to Gladstone, a Dingle service rounds the curve and rumbles to a halt.

Above top 1891 North of Alexandra, the line left Regent Road with successive left and right curves and continued to hug the dockside. Sailing ships dominate the scene in the distant and relatively new Hornby Dock (built 1884). On the right can be seen part of the Lancashire & Yorkshire Railway's North Mersey Goods Yard which was laid out in 1867.

Above 1930s At Gladstone, passengers spill onto the platform and can see which Canadian Pacific, Blue Funnel, White Star or United States Lines ships are on display. Vessels at this dock frequently sailed for ports such as Adelaide, Albany, Boston, Brisbane, Cape Town, Dunedin, Fremantle, Halifax, Lyttleton, Melbourne, Montreal, New York, Philadelphia, Quebec, St Johns and Sydney. The large crane on the opposite side was the one employed in the ex-LYR North Mersey goods yard.

Above top 1930s The last of the White Star liners, *Britannic* in port. Although now owned by Cunard, she retained her buff and black funnels and was festooned with flags from stem to stern. Built by Harland and Wolff, she made her maiden voyage from Liverpool to New York in June 1930. This luxurious vessel was one of the last great liners to visit the city in a truly working capacity and it seems fitting her final voyage ended at Liverpool in December 1960.

Above 1930s The Canadian Pacific steamship *Duchess of Athol* at the dockside. She was one of four such vessels detailed to Liverpool, her sister ships being *Duchess of Bedford*, *Duchess of York* and *Duchess of Richmond*.

Opposite top 1930s In another part of Gladstone the huge floating crane *Hercules* is at work alongside *Pacific Ranger* of Norfolk & North American Shipping Co. which was managed by the Furness Withy Co. Sandwiched between this vessel and the quayside is *New Zealand Star* of the Blue Star Line.

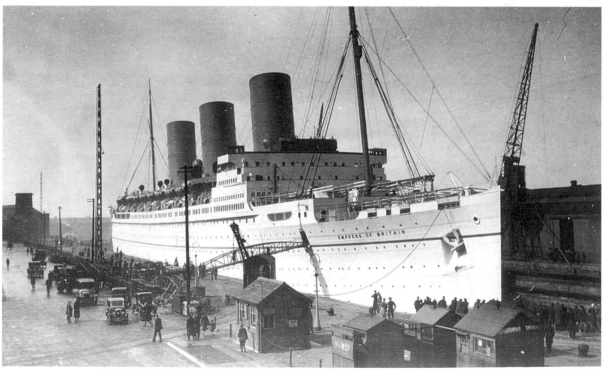

Above 1930s Further north in the dry dock, we see the 42,500 ton *Empress of Britain*, a magnificent white vessel with three huge buff-coloured funnels. This was the largest of the Canadian Pacific fleet and the last word in luxury sailing. A favourite of royalty and film stars alike, she cost a massive £3 million and was consistently referred to as 'Mayfair afloat' following her maiden voyage in 1931. Sadly, the reign of this wonderful Empress was cut short by a German U-boat in 1940. She was the largest merchant ship sunk during World War Two, falling prey on the homeward bound leg of a round trip to Suez from Liverpool – 598 of her passengers and crew were rescued but a total of 49 perished.

Above top 1930s The view north from Gladstone station footbridge. In the distance the line curves inland to Seaforth whilst, on the right, piles of imported timber in the North Mersey goods yard testify to the depot's chief commodity.

Above and opposite top 1930s On board a train for Seaforth Sands an elevated view of another Canadian Pacific ship, *Duchess of Richmond*, a 20,000 tonner of 1928 vintage. This vessel did sterling work in the Second World War and was renamed *Empress of Canada* after a refurbishment in 1947. Its new identity was not a lucky one, however, as it caught fire while berthed at Gladstone in 1953, keeled over and became a total loss despite valiant attempts by many fire-crews. The photograph opposite shows the salvaged hull being made seaworthy prior to towing to a breaker's yard in Italy.

Opposite bottom 1930s Rounding the curve on the approach to Seaforth a final view of Gladstone dry dock and another liner in residence, this time *Mauretania* of the Cunard fleet, with a throng of admirers at her bow.

Above & opposite top 1892, 1923, 1933 The approach to Seaforth Sands over three different decades. When first constructed, the station was a decorative but relatively straightforward terminus. Also note that the current in those days was collected from a centre rail. Some 31 years later the 'through' station was added to allow trains to continue to the LMS station at Seaforth & Litherland (although the rail link was actually in place from 1905). The last picture shows the approach eight years after the terminus had been dismantled in favour of a carriage shed and workshop.

Above 1956 Trains at Seaforth Sands. The clearance was not great between widened carriages such as these and it was not recommended for passengers to put their heads out of the window for a better view.

Above top 1930s Seaforth Sands station twenty years earlier.
Above 1930 A train crosses the bridge towards Seaforth & Litherland at the junction of Crosby Road South and Seaforth Road. The posters below advertise cinematic opportunities at the 'Stella' and the soon to be opened 'Carlton Talkie Theatre'. The former boasted the very latest 'RCA' sound equipment to enhance everyone's enjoyment of *Paris* and *The Girl from Woolworths*.

1956 In Seaforth train shed, a marriage of old and new carriages which were salvaged from the malicious fire at Sands station earlier that year when sets of original and modernised stock were engulfed.

Above 1956 A diminutive Ruston diesel locomotive used only for engineering work. It was bought by the company in 1947 to replace a similarly sized steam engine.

Opposite top 1930s An elevated walkway leads directly from the works to the station. The line descending to the North Mersey goods yard can be seen on the far left of this photograph.

Opposite bottom c.1900 The original station at the turn of the century on the occasion of Seaforth Fair, only a fraction of which is visible here. This well attended annual event was staged on the triangle of waste land bounded by Seaforth Road, the railway embankment and Beaumaris Street. The headings on the station billboards opposite are noteworthy as they represent no fewer that seven different railway companies (l to r) L&NW Ry, Midland Ry, Mersey Ry, Liverpool Overhead Ry, Cheshire Lines, Gt.Western Ry and L&Y Ry.

Opposite 1930s Rimrose Road Junction signal box. An Aintree race-day special train would have crossed over here to the North Mersey branch, pictured right.

Above Having negotiated the curve we pull into Seaforth & Litherland station on the Liverpool – Southport line. The end of our journey is but a few yards away.

SPECIAL
SEAFORTH SANDS
SEAFORTH L.M.S.
FOR SOUTHPORT LINE
DINGLE
PIER HEAD
JAMES STREET
HUSKISSON
CANADA
CLARENCE
HERCULANEUM
AINTREE
SOUTHPORT
GLADSTONE
TOXTETH

Opposite top 1953,
Opposite bottom 1930s
Journey's end, Seaforth &
Litherland. We alight from
the carriage and descend
the steps which lead us to
Seaforth Road.
Left A destination blind
from a modernised unit,
fully extended to reveal a
curious range of locations.
Apart from the weathered
top trio, the only other
ones likely to have seen
active service were
Pier Head, Herculaneum
and Aintree.